GUITAR PLAY-ALONG

AUDIO
ACCESS
INCLUDED

ROCK POP

PLAYBACK+
Speed • Pitch • Balance • Loop

To access audio visit:
www.halleonard.com/mylibrary

Enter Code
3351-8728-2364-4585

ISBN 978-1-5400-4941-4

Visit Hal Leonard Online at
www.halleonard.com

Contact us:
Hal Leonard
7777 West Bluemound Road
Milwaukee, WI 53213
Email: info@halleonard.com

In Europe, contact:
Hal Leonard Europe Limited
42 Wigmore Street
Marylebone, London, W1U 2RN
Email: info@halleonardeurope.com

In Australia, contact:
Hal Leonard Australia Pty. Ltd.
4 Lentara Court
Cheltenham, Victoria, 3192 Australia
Email: info@halleonard.com.au

CONTENTS

GUITAR NOTATION LEGEND

THE MUSICAL STAFF shows pitches and rhythms and is divided by bar lines into measures. Pitches are named after the first seven letters of the alphabet.

TABLATURE graphically represents the guitar fingerboard. Each horizontal line represents a string, and each number represents a fret.

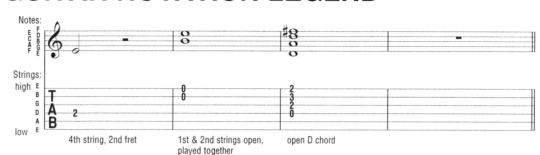

4th string, 2nd fret | 1st & 2nd strings open, played together | open D chord

HALF-STEP BEND: Strike the note and bend up 1/2 step.

WHOLE-STEP BEND: Strike the note and bend up one step.

GRACE NOTE BEND: Strike the note and immediately bend up as indicated.

SLIGHT (MICROTONE) BEND: Strike the note and bend up 1/4 step.

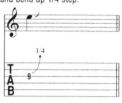

BEND AND RELEASE: Strike the note and bend up as indicated, then release back to the original note. Only the first note is struck.

PRE-BEND: Bend the note as indicated, then strike it.

VIBRATO: The string is vibrated by rapidly bending and releasing the note with the fretting hand.

PALM MUTING: The note is partially muted by the pick hand lightly touching the string(s) just before the bridge.

HAMMER-ON: Strike the first (lower) note with one finger, then sound the higher note (on the same string) with another finger by fretting it without picking.

PULL-OFF: Place both fingers on the notes to be sounded. Strike the first note and without picking, pull the finger off to sound the second (lower) note.

LEGATO SLIDE: Strike the first note and then slide the same fret-hand finger up or down to the second note. The second note is not struck.

SHIFT SLIDE: Same as legato slide, except the second note is struck.

TRILL: Very rapidly alternate between the notes indicated by continuously hammering on and pulling off.

TAPPING: Hammer ("tap") the fret indicated with the pick-hand index or middle finger and pull off to the note fretted by the fret hand.

NATURAL HARMONIC: Strike the note while the fret-hand lightly touches the string directly over the fret indicated.

PINCH HARMONIC: The note is fretted normally and a harmonic is produced by adding the edge of the thumb or the tip of the index finger of the pick hand to the normal pick attack.

TREMOLO PICKING: The note is picked as rapidly and continuously as possible.

VIBRATO BAR DIVE AND RETURN: The pitch of the note or chord is dropped a specified number of steps (in rhythm), then returned to the original pitch.

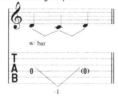

VIBRATO BAR SCOOP: Depress the bar just before striking the note, then quickly release the bar.

VIBRATO BAR DIP: Strike the note and then immediately drop a specified number of steps, then release back to the original pitch.

Additional Musical Definitions

(accent) • Accentuate note (play it louder).

(staccato) • Play the note short.

D.S. al Coda • Go back to the sign (%), then play until the measure marked *"To Coda,"* then skip to the section labelled "Coda."

D.C. al Fine • Go back to the beginning of the song and play until the measure marked *"Fine"* (end).

Fill • Label used to identify a brief melodic figure which is to be inserted into the arrangement.

N.C. • Harmony is implied.

 • Repeat measures between signs.

 • When a repeated section has different endings, play the first ending only the first time and the second ending only the second time.

Every Breath You Take

Music and Lyrics by Sting

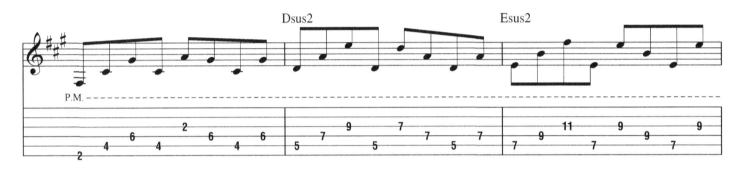

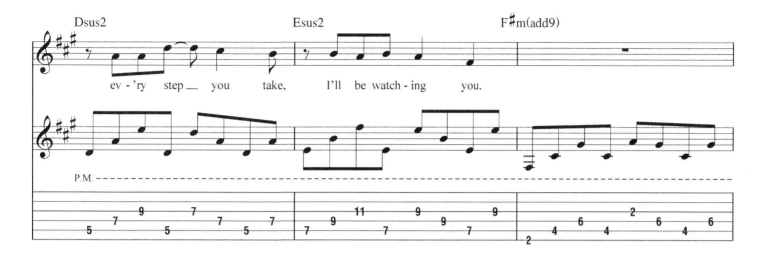

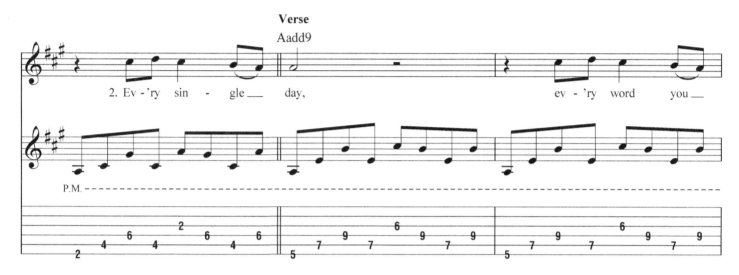

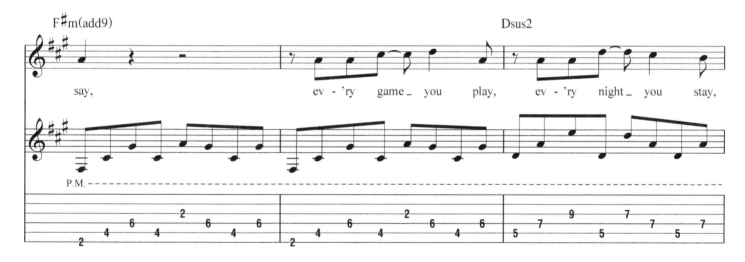

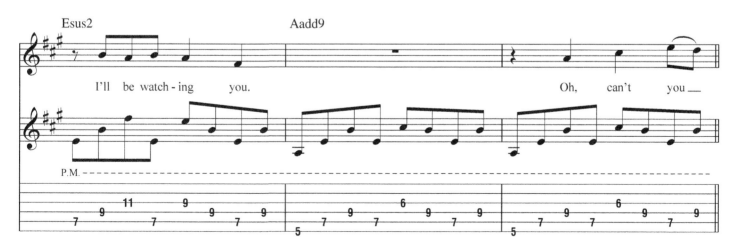

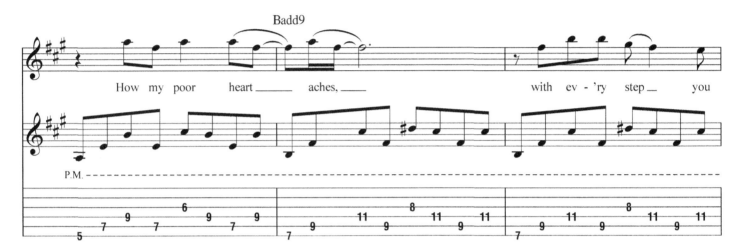

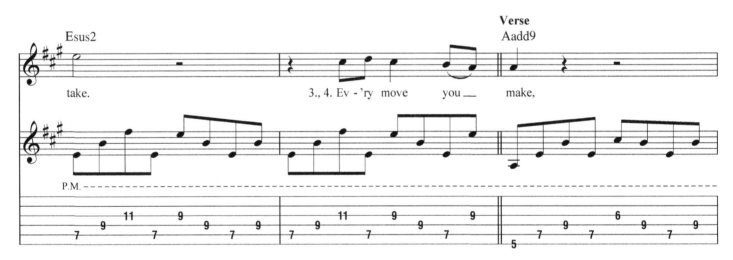

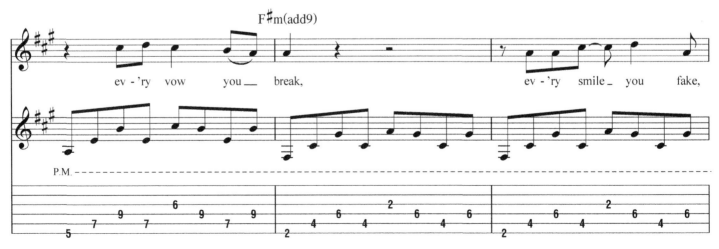

Interlude

I keep cry - ing, ba - by, ba - by, please.

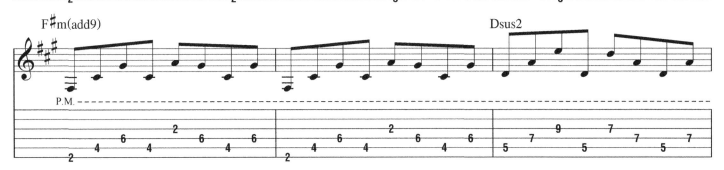

D.S. al Coda

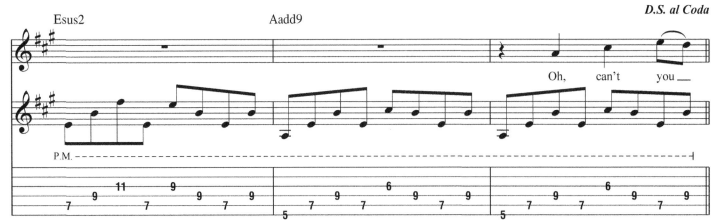

Oh, can't you

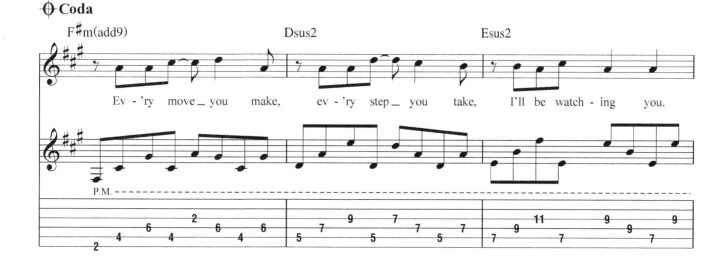

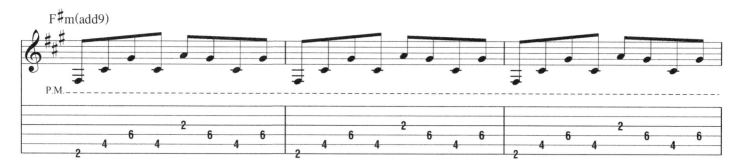

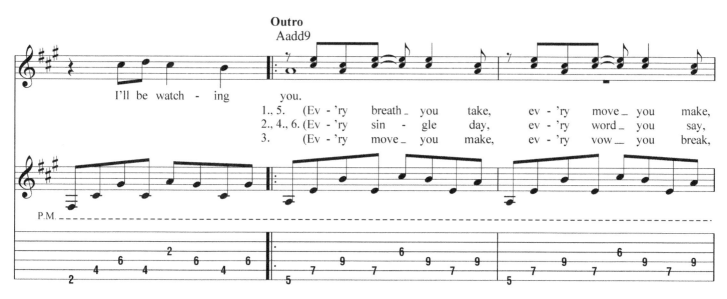

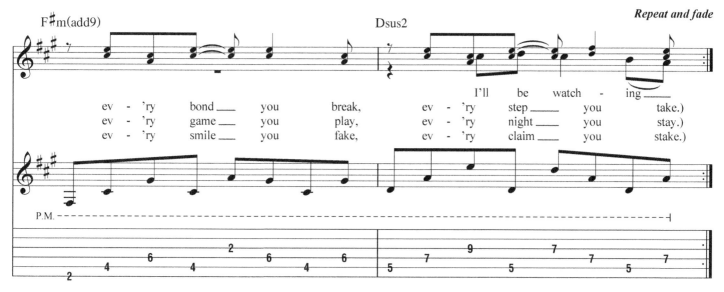

Heartbreaker

Words and Music by Cliff Wade and Geoff Gill

Intro
Moderately ♩ = 156

1. Your love is like a tid - al wave
2. *See additional lyrics*

spin - nin' o - ver my head. Drown - in' me in your prom -

- is - es better left un - said.

You're the right kind of sin - ner to re - lease my in - ner fan -

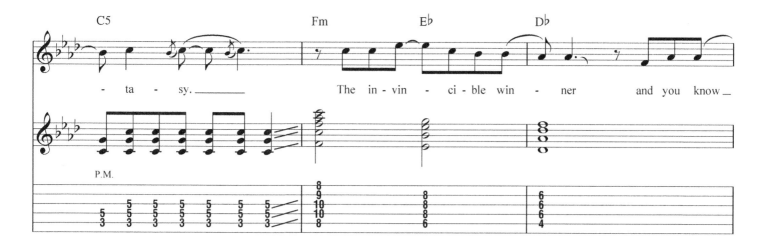

- ta - sy.____ The in - vin - ci - ble win - ner and you know__

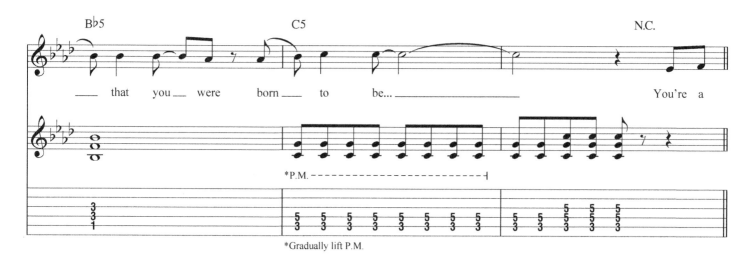

__ that you __ were born __ to be... ____ You're a

*Gradually lift P.M.

Chorus

heart - break - er,____ dream mak - er,____ love tak - er, don't you

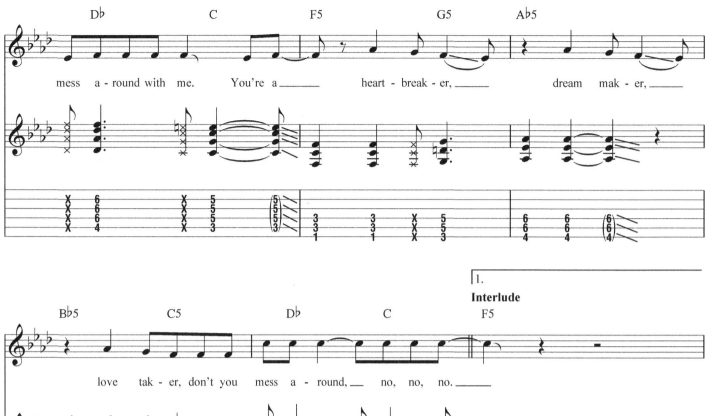

mess a-round with me. You're a _____ heart-break-er, _____ dream mak-er, _____

1.

Interlude

love tak-er, don't you mess a-round, __ no, no, no. _____

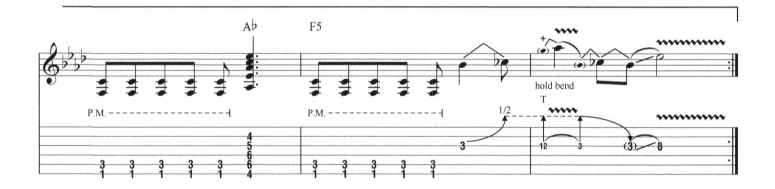

2.

Interlude

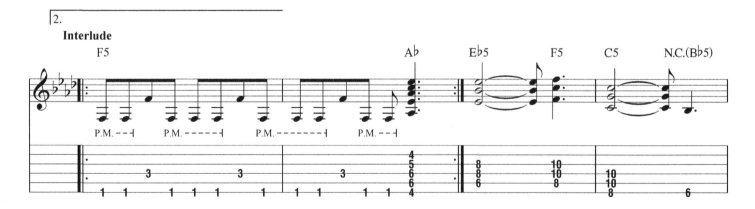

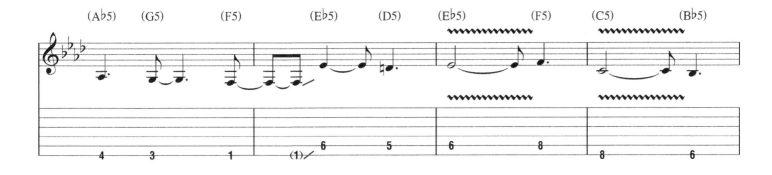

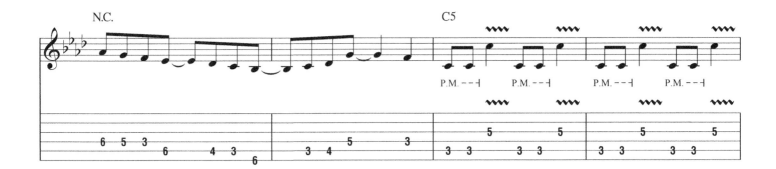

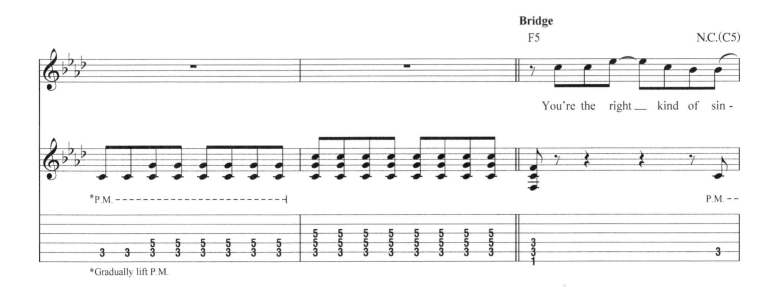

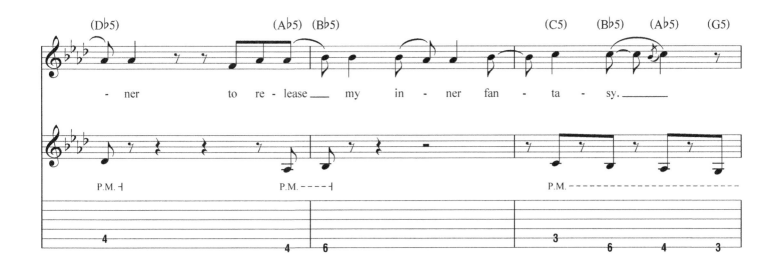

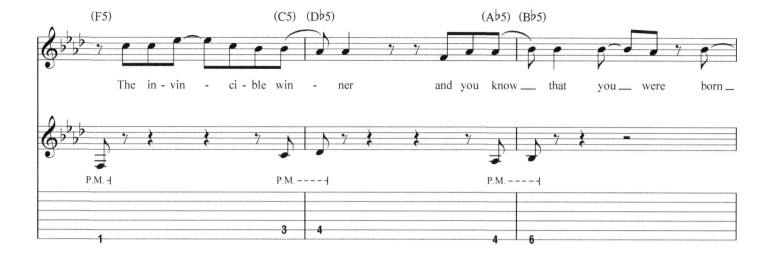

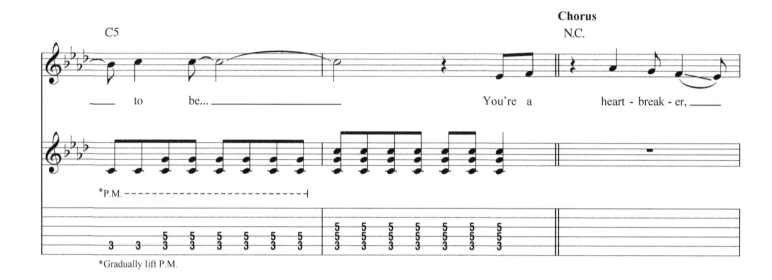

*Gradually lift P.M.

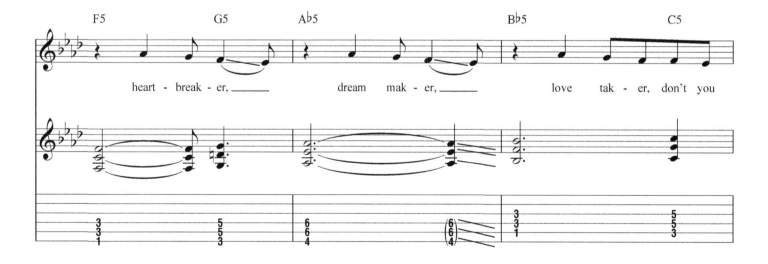

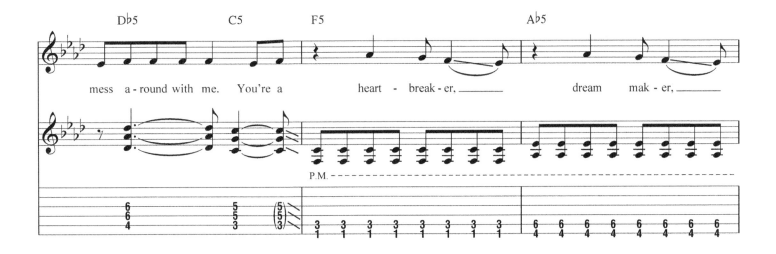

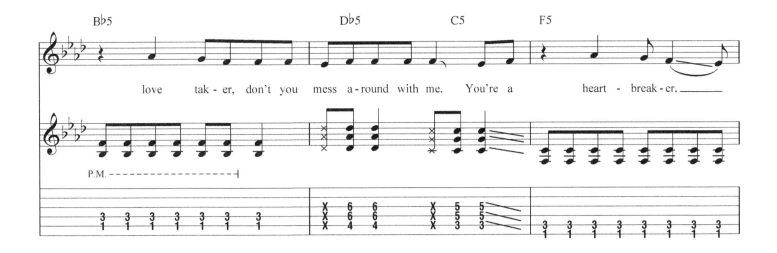

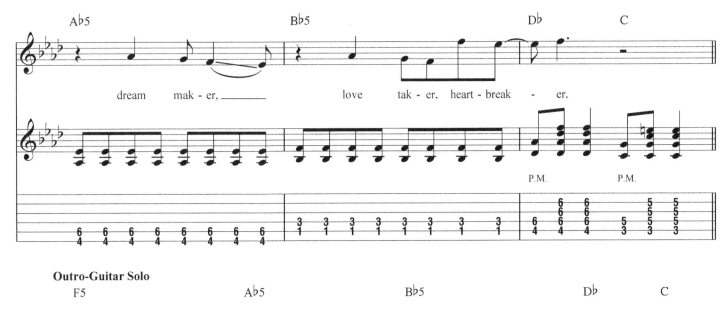

Outro-Guitar Solo

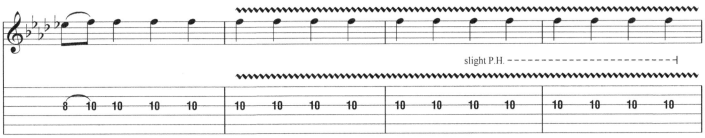

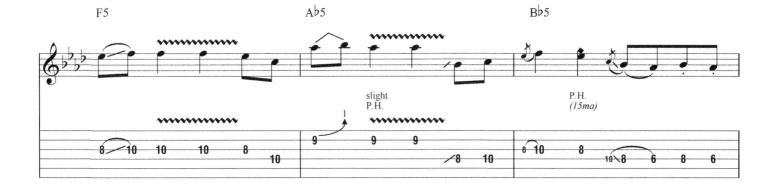

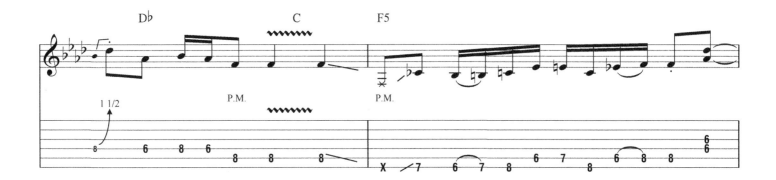

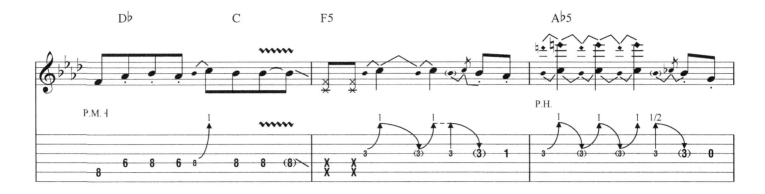

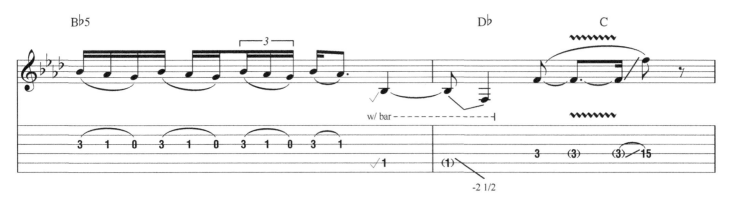

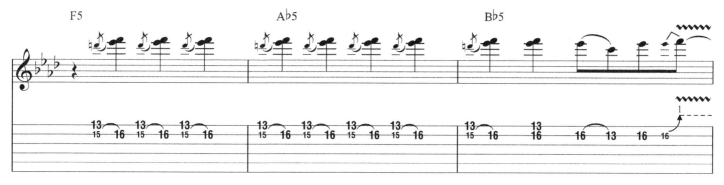

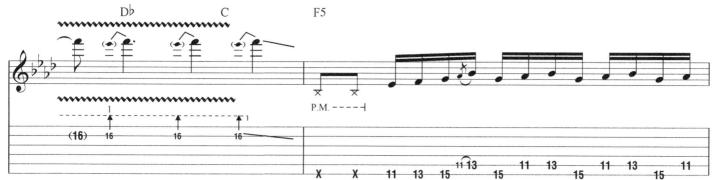

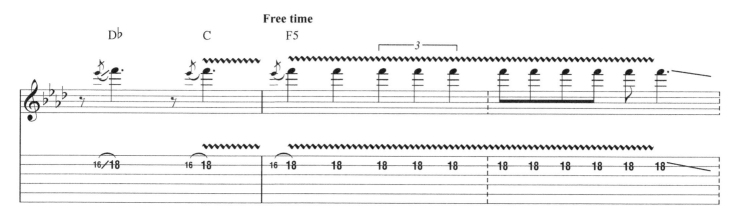

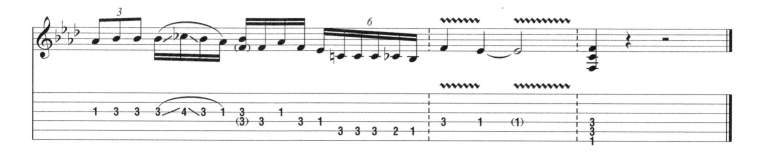

Additional Lyrics

2. Your love has set my soul on fire, burning out of control.
You taught me the ways of desire, now it's taken it's toll.

Hot Blooded

Words and Music by Mick Jones and Lou Gramm

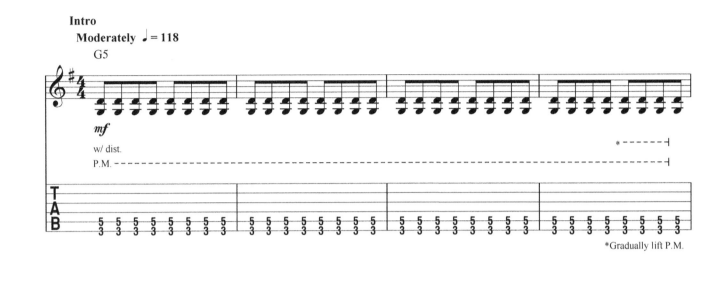

*Gradually lift P.M.

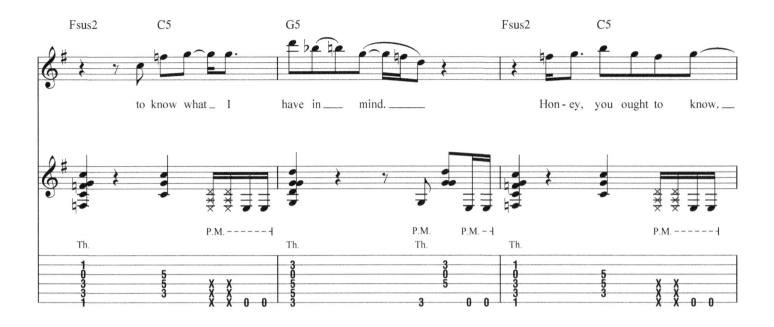

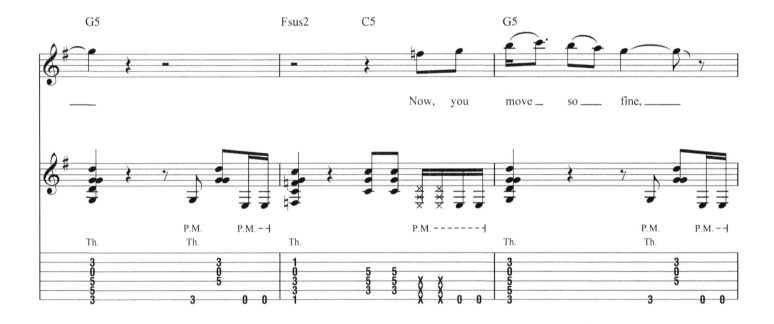

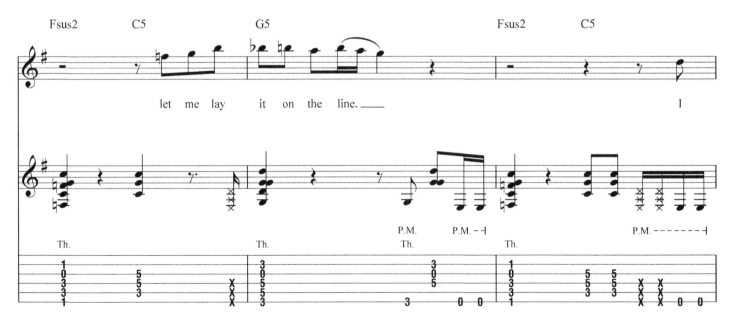

Pre-Chorus

I'll show you lov- in' like ___ you ___ nev- er knew. ___ That's why I'm

⊕ Coda 1

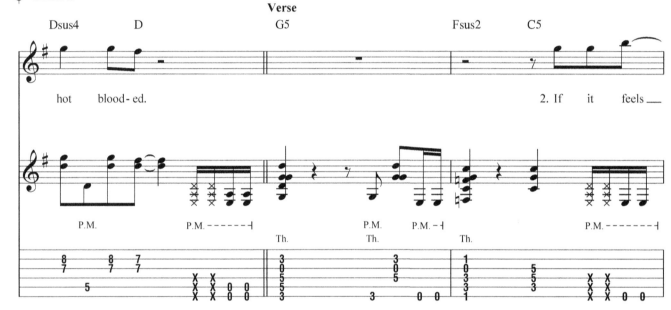

Verse

hot blood- ed. 2. If it feels ___

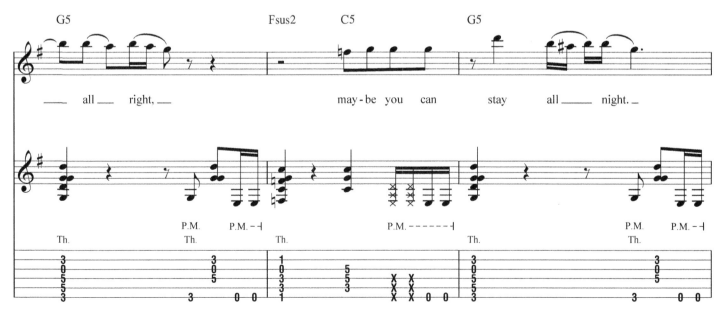

___ all ___ right, ___ may- be you can stay all ___ night. ___

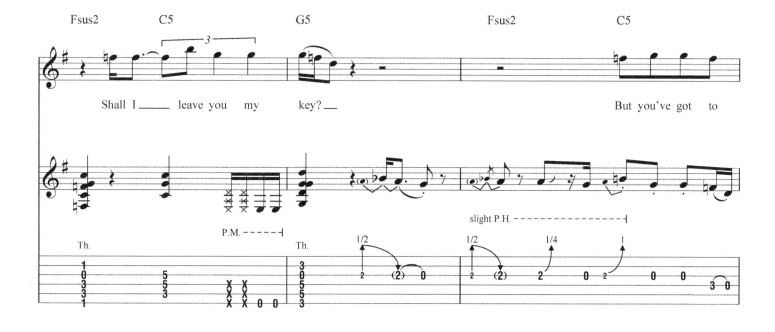

Shall I ___ leave you my key? ___ But you've got to

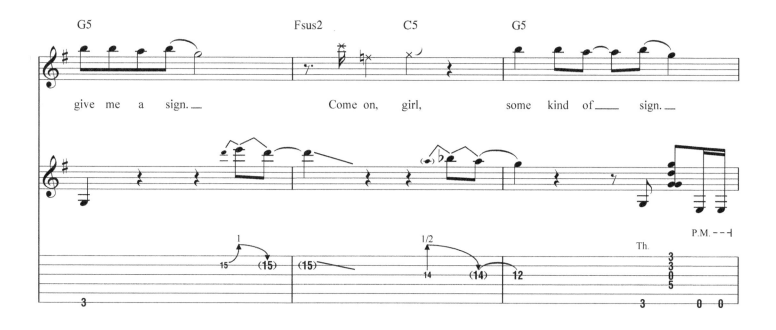

give me a sign. ___ Come on, girl, some kind of ___ sign. ___

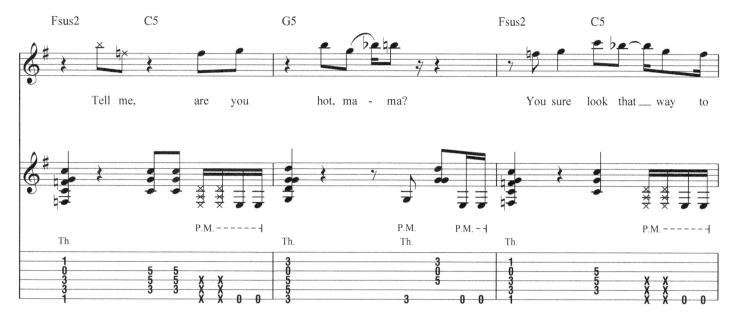

Tell me, are you hot, ma - ma? You sure look that ___ way to

Guitar Solo

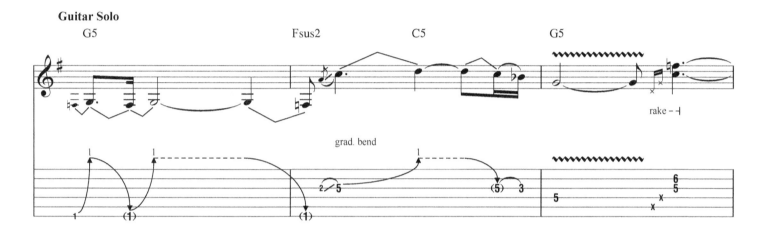

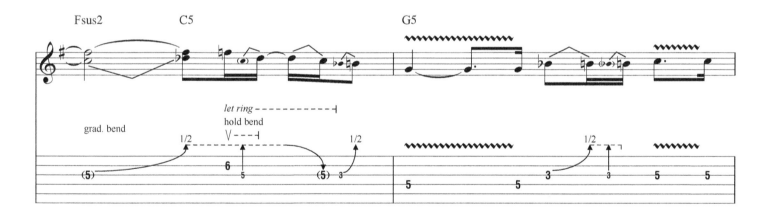

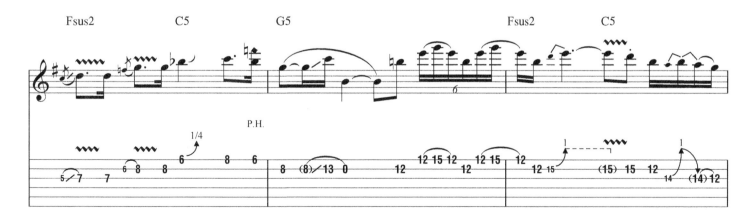

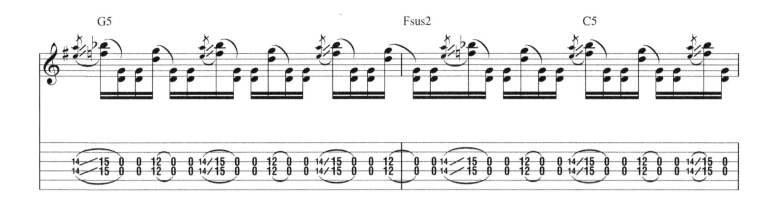

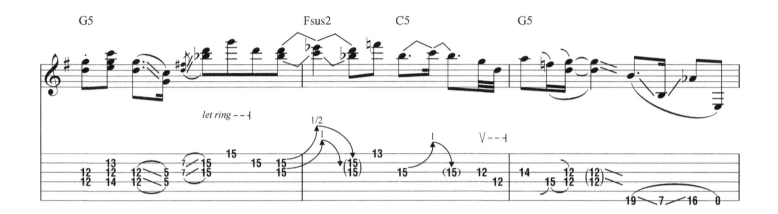

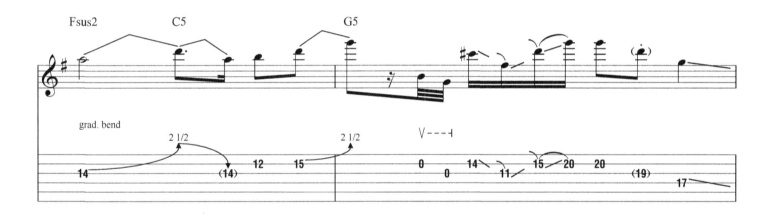

Pre-Chorus

Now it's up to you. ___ Can we make a se - cret

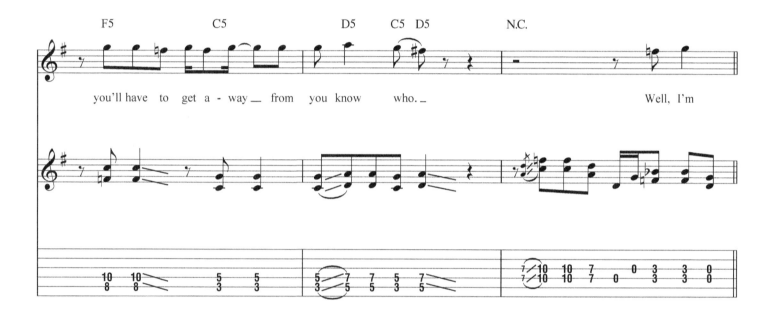

Outro-Chorus

w/ Voc. ad lib on repeats

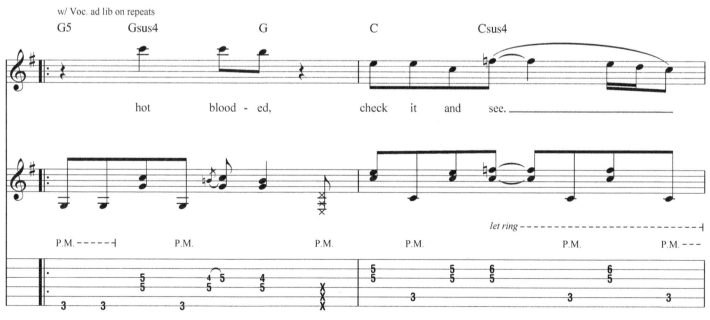

I got a fe - ver of a hun - dred and three. ___

Come on, ba - by, do you do more than dance?

Repeat and fade

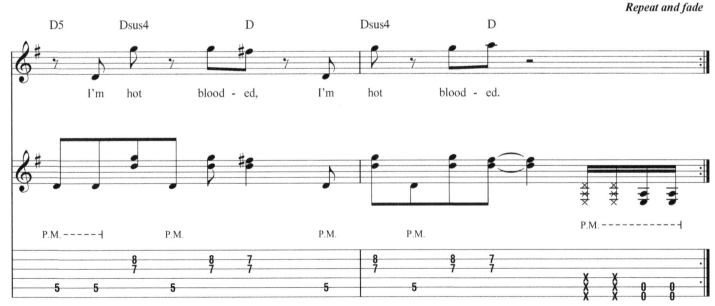

I'm hot blood - ed, I'm hot blood - ed.

Money for Nothing

Words and Music by Mark Knopfler and Sting

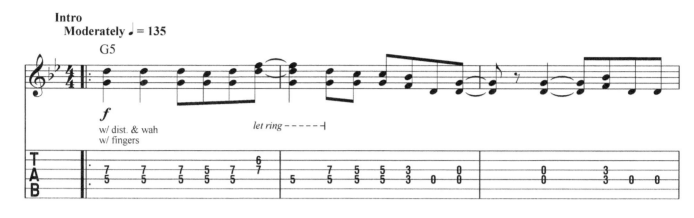

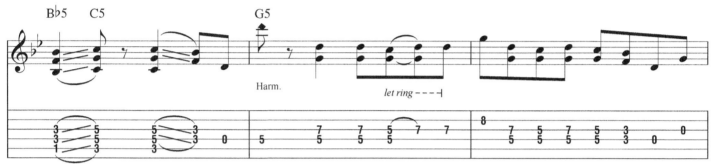

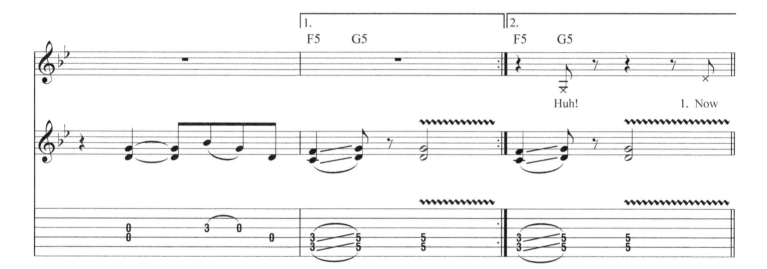

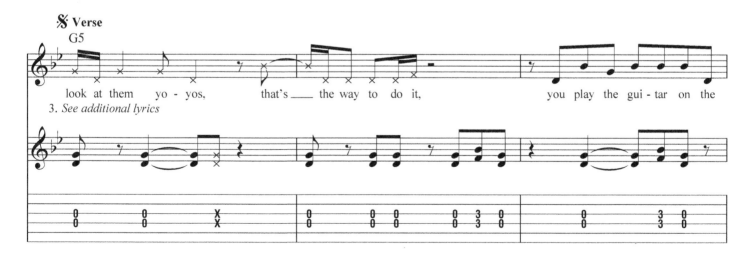

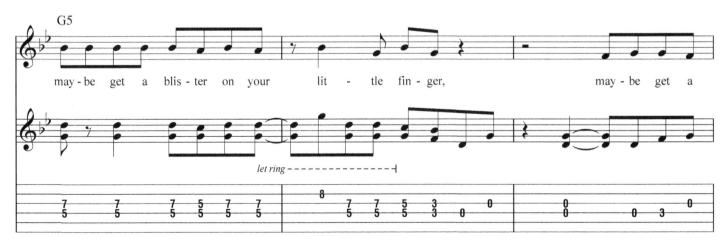

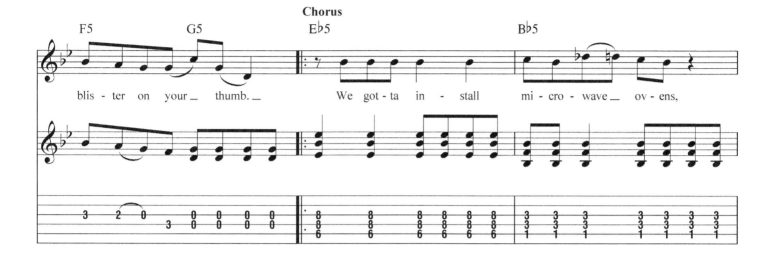

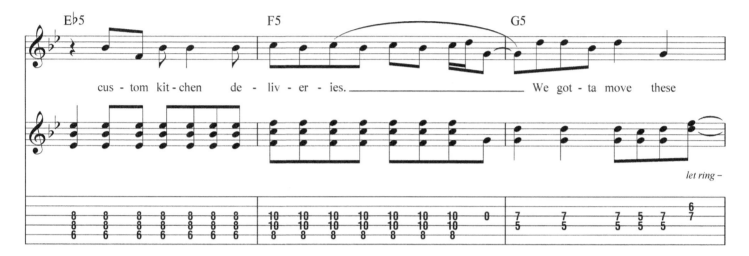

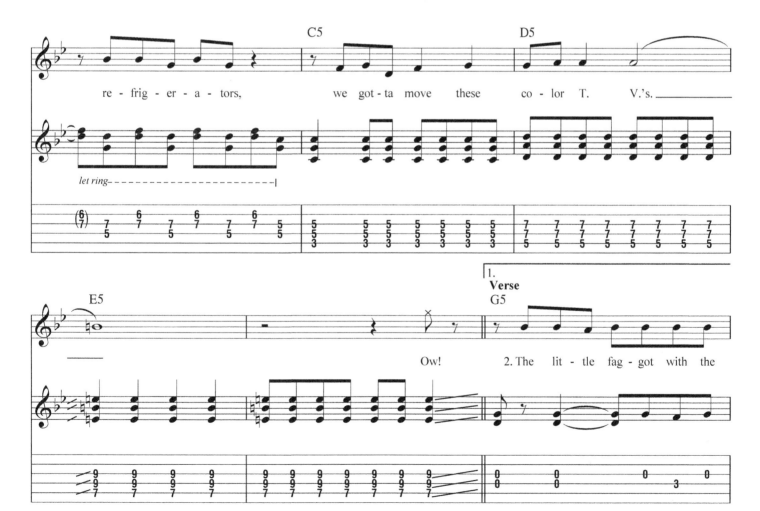

ear - ring and the make - up, yeah, bud - dy, that's his own hair.

That lit - tle fag - got got his own jet air - plane, that lit - tle fag - got, he's a

Interlude

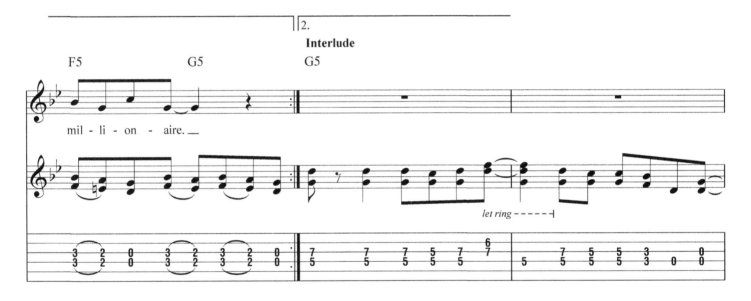

mil - li - on - aire.

let ring

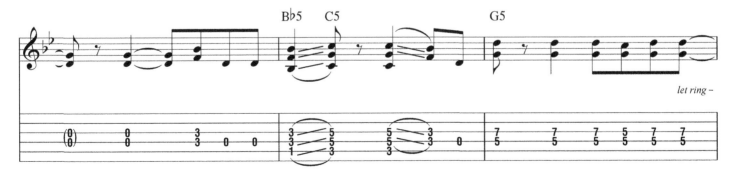

let ring –

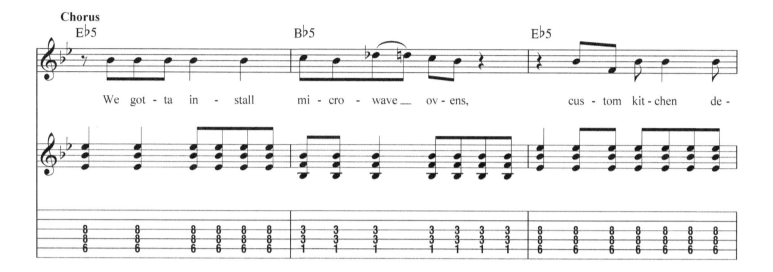

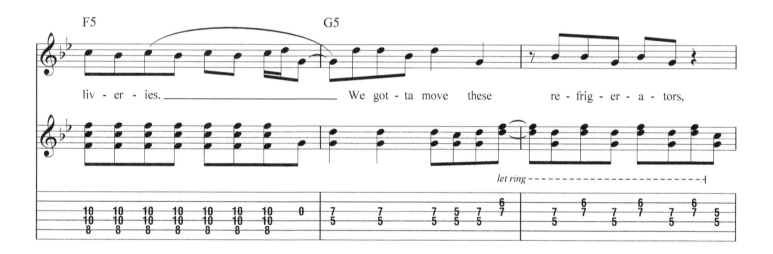

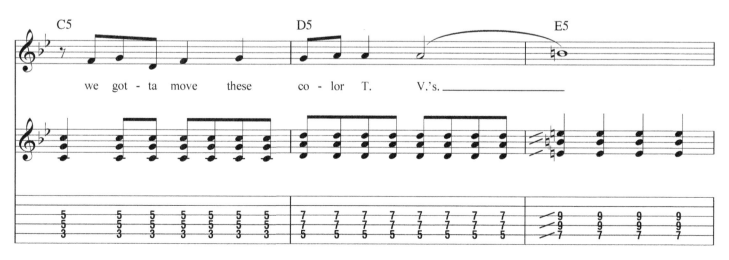

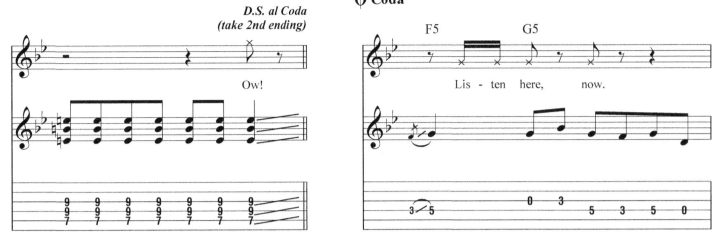

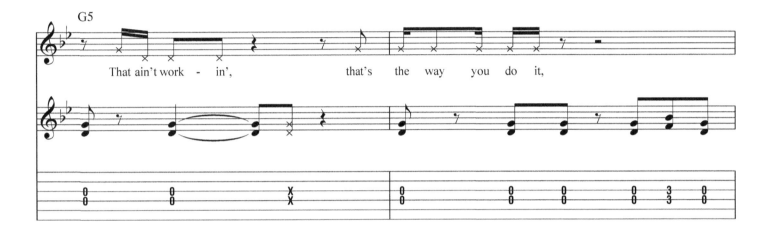

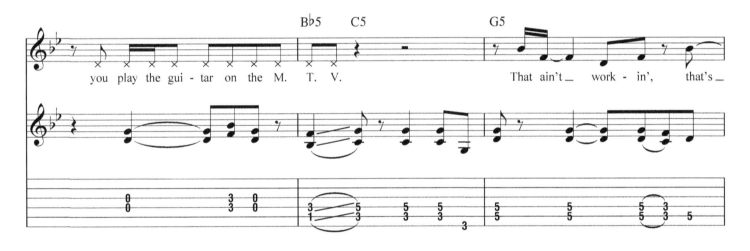

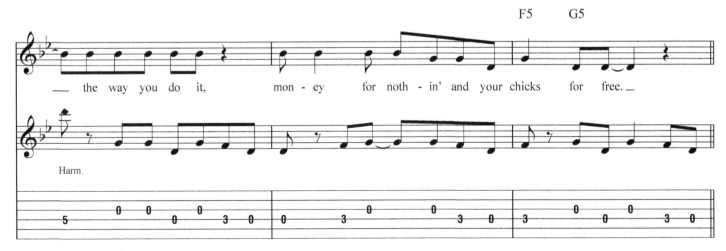

Outro

Mon - ey for noth - in' and your

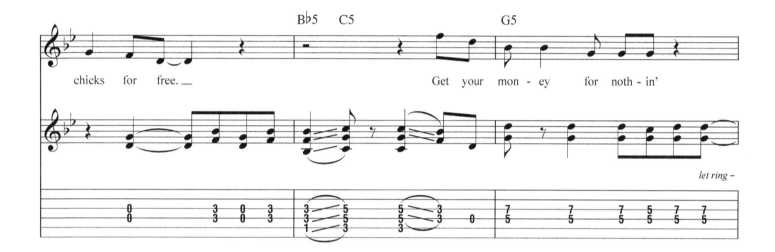

chicks for free. Get your mon - ey for noth - in'

let ring –

Repeat and fade

and your chicks for free.

let ring - - - -

Additional Lyrics

3. I should have learned to play the guitar,
   I should have learned to play them drums.
   Look at that mama, she got it stickin' in the cameraman.
   We could have some fun.
   And he's up there, what's that? Hawaiian noises?
   He's bangin' on the bongos like a chimpanzee.
   Oh, that ain't workin', that's the way to do it.
   Get your money for nothing, get your chicks for free.

Jessie's Girl

Words and Music by Rick Springfield

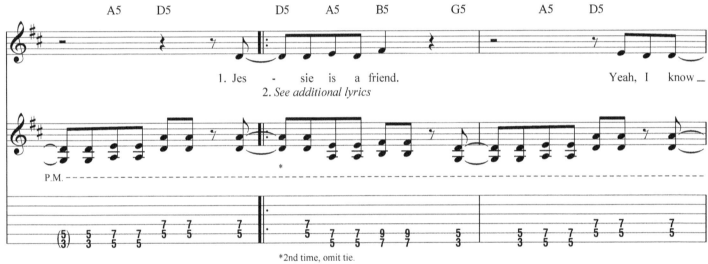

Tell me... Where can I find a wom-an like that?

Guitar Solo

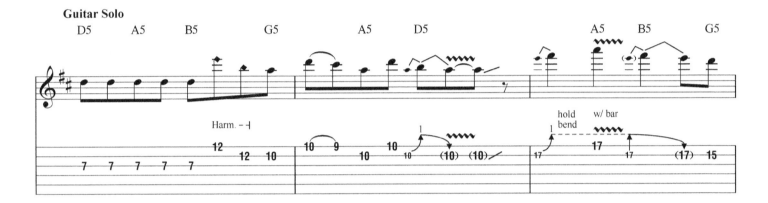

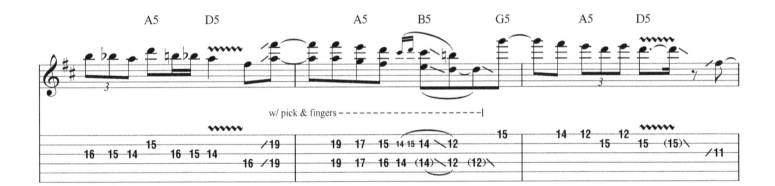

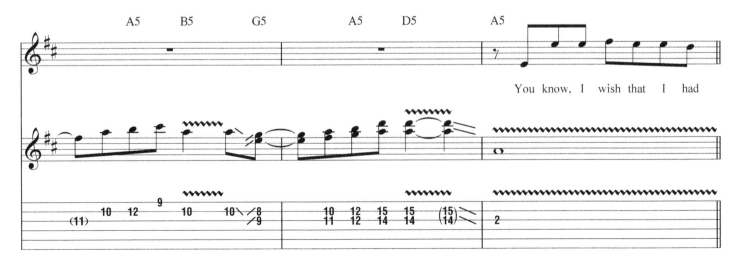

You know, I wish that I had

Chorus

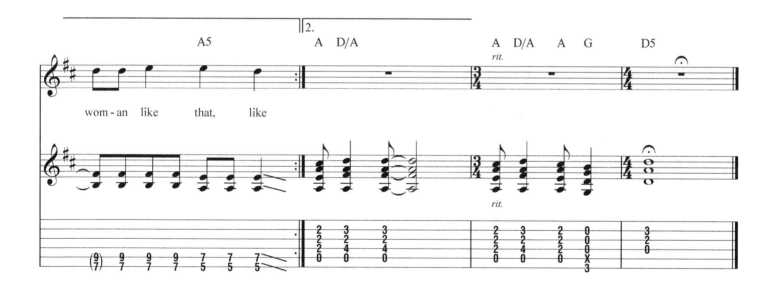

Additional Lyrics

2. I'll play along with this charade.
   There doesn't seem to be a reason to change.
   You know, I feel so dirty when they start talkin' cute.
   I wanna tell her that I love her, but the point is prob'ly moot.
   'Cause she's...

Pour Some Sugar on Me

Words and Music by Joe Elliott, Phil Collen, Richard Savage, Richard Allen, Steve Clark and R.J. Lange

Look-in' like a tramp, like a vid-e-o vamp. Dem-o-li-tion wom-an, can I be your man? (Your

man. Hey! Hey!)

Raz-zle and a daz-zle and a flash a lit-tle light. Tel-e-vi-sion lov-er, ba-by, go all night.

Some-time, an-y-time, sug-ar me sweet. Lit-tle miss in-no-cent, sug-ar me. Yeah.__

Yeah. ___ Come on.

※ Pre-Chorus

Take the bot - tle, ___ shake it up. ___

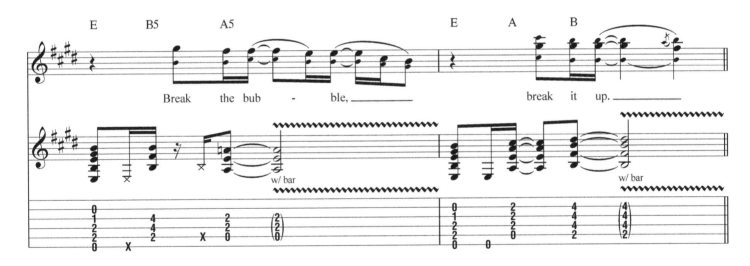

Break the bub - ble, ___ break it up. ___

Chorus

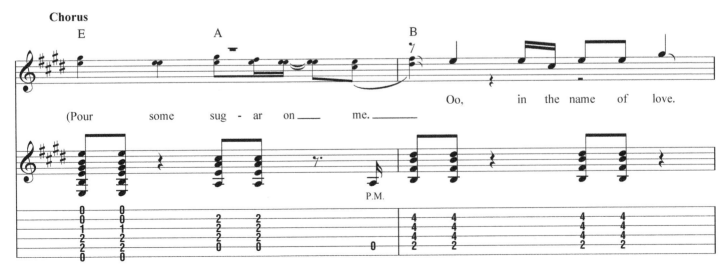

Oo, in the name of love.
(Pour some sug - ar on ___ me.

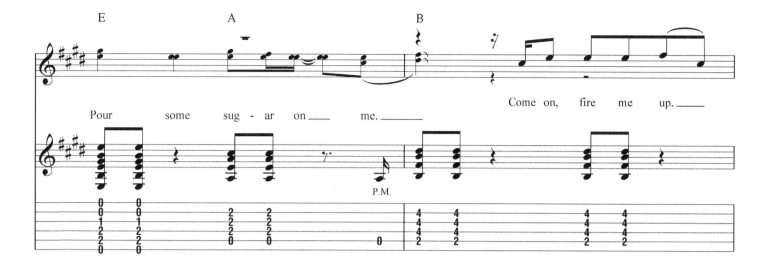

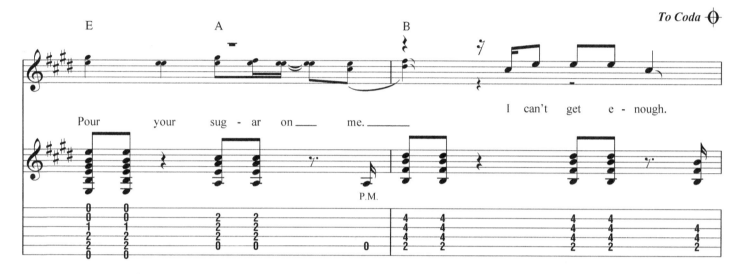

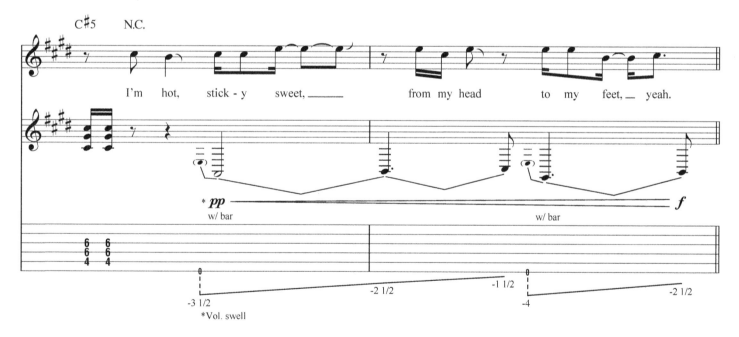

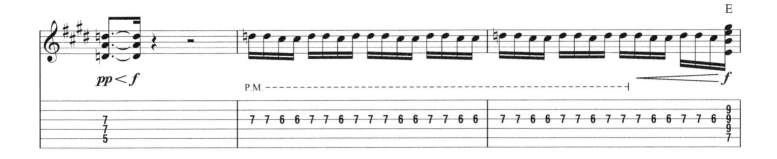

Bridge

Gtr. tacet

Sweet to taste. _ 'Cause I'm

(You got the peach - es, I _ got the cream.

Sac - cha - rin. _

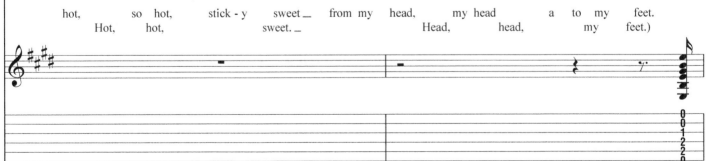

hot, so hot, stick - y sweet _ from my head, my head a to my feet.

Hot, hot, sweet. _ Head, head, my feet.)

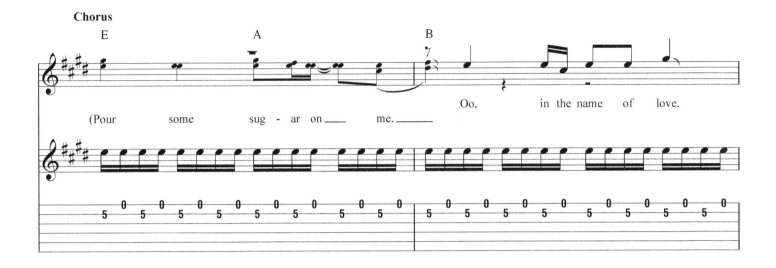

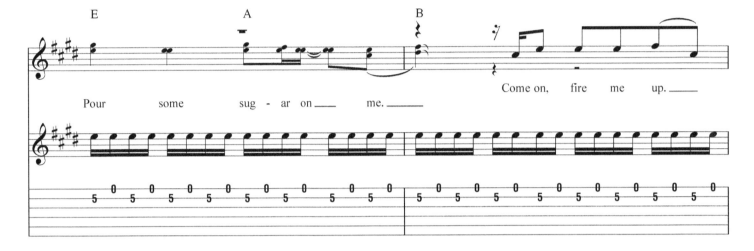

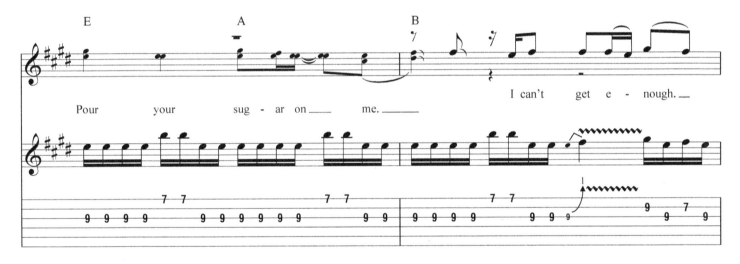

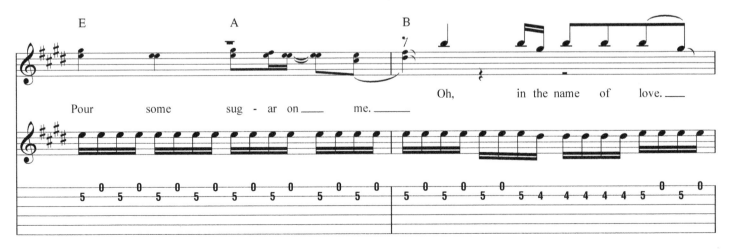

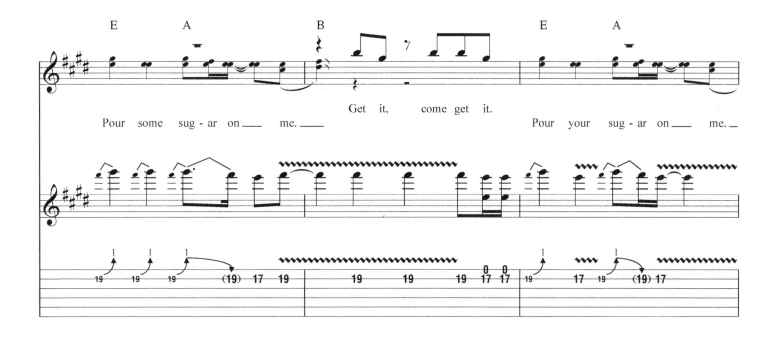

Pour some sug - ar on ___ me. ___ Get it, come get it. Pour your sug - ar on ___ me. ___

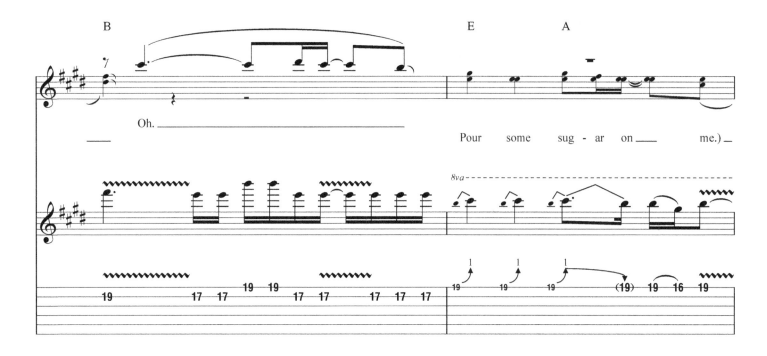

Oh. ___ Pour some sug - ar on ___ me.) __

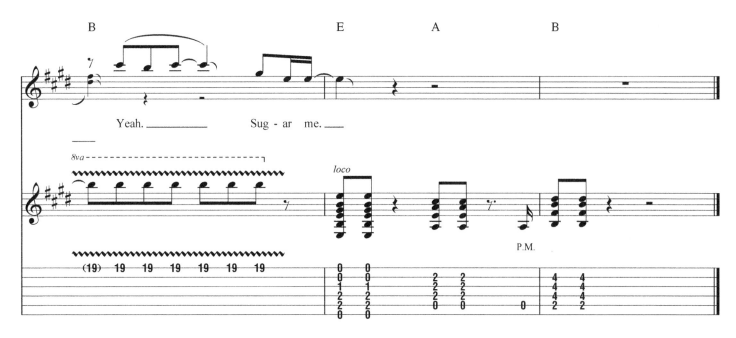

Yeah. ___ Sug - ar me. ___

Separate Ways
(Worlds Apart)

Words and Music by Steve Perry and Jonathan Cain

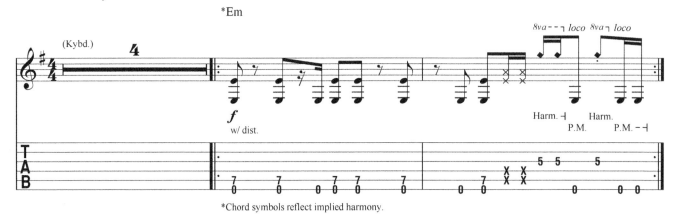

*Chord symbols reflect implied harmony.

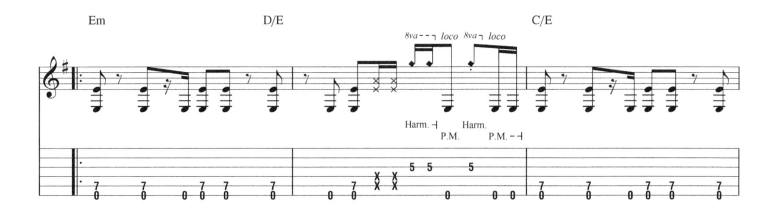

worlds a - part, ___ hearts bro - ken in two, two, _

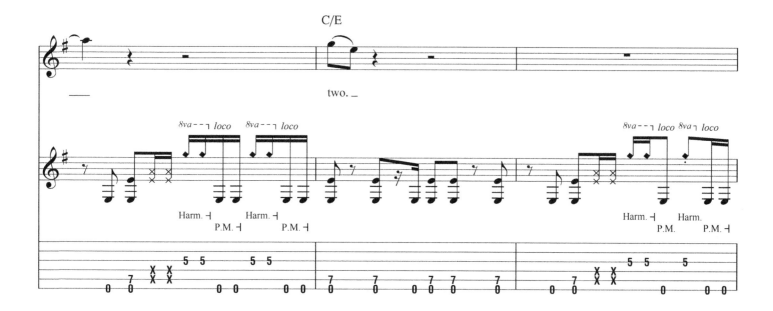

two. _

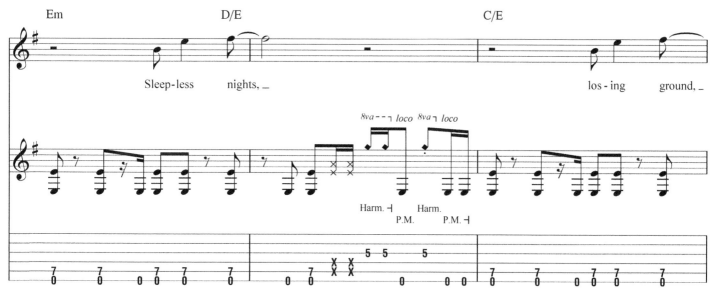

Sleep-less nights, _ los - ing ground, _

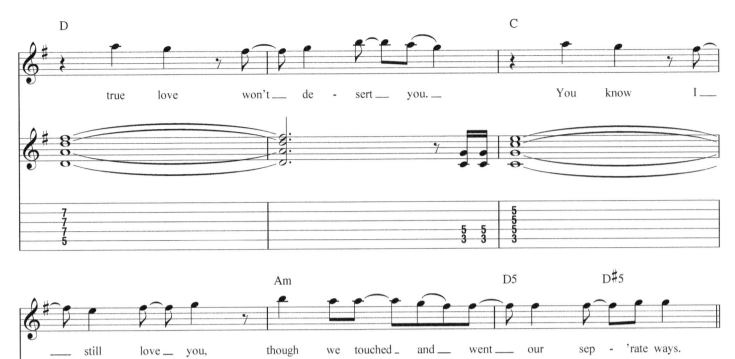

D   C

true love won't de - sert you.   You know I

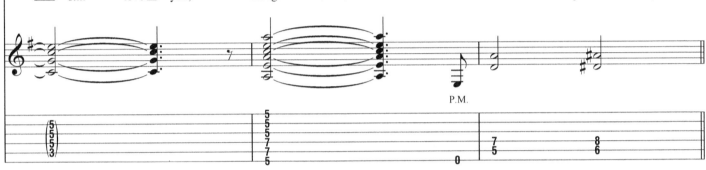

Am   D5   D#5

still love you, though we touched and went our sep - 'rate ways.

P.M.

Interlude

Em   D/E   C/E

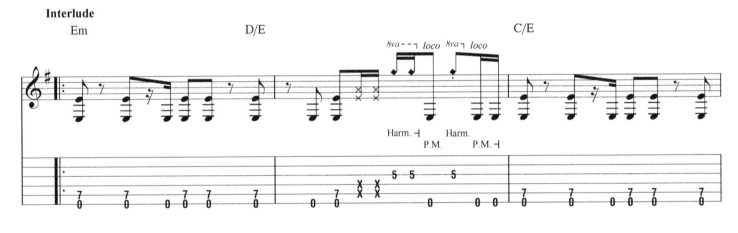

1.   2.   **Verse**

Em   D/E

2. Trou - bled   times,

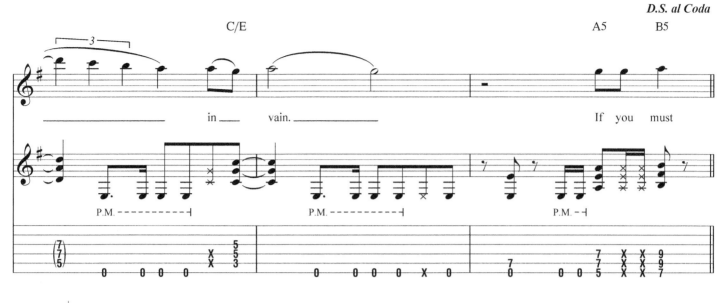

in __ vain. _____ If you must

⊕ Coda

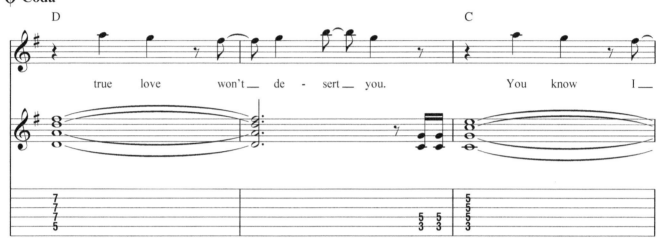

true love won't __ de - sert __ you. You know I __

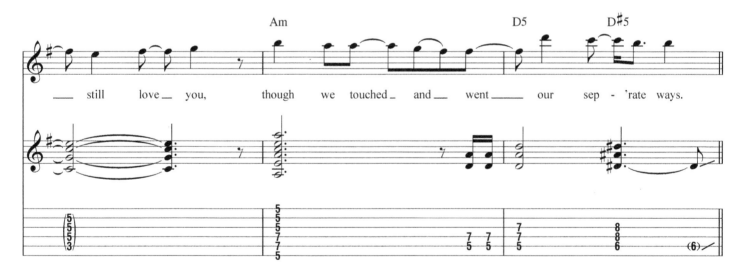

__ still love __ you, though we touched __ and __ went _____ our sep - 'rate ways.

Guitar Solo

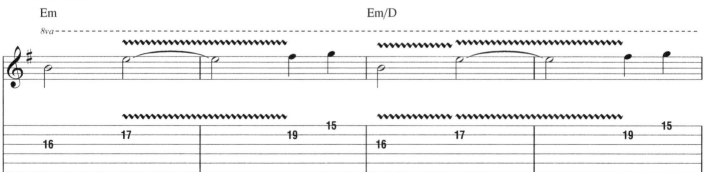

Interlude

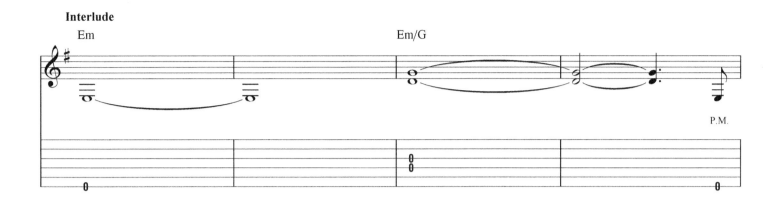

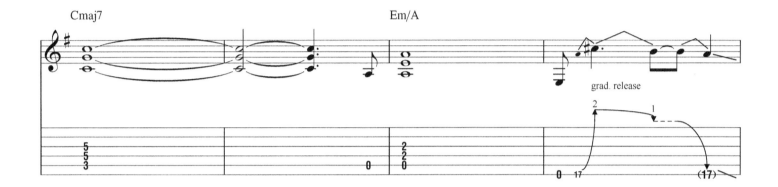

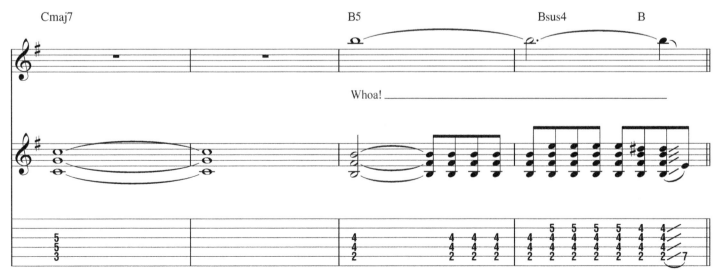

Some - day love ___ will find ___ you, break those chains ___

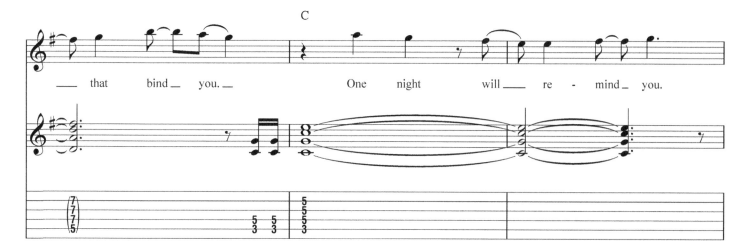

___ that bind ___ you. ___ One night will ___ re - mind _ you.

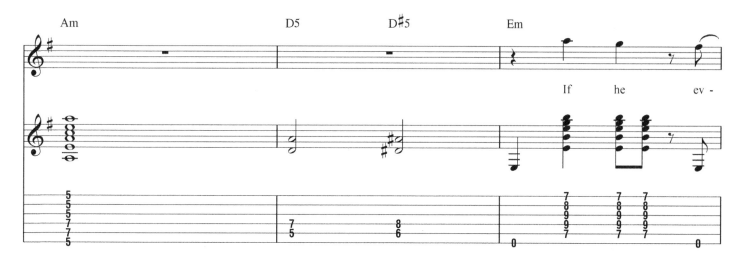

If he ev -

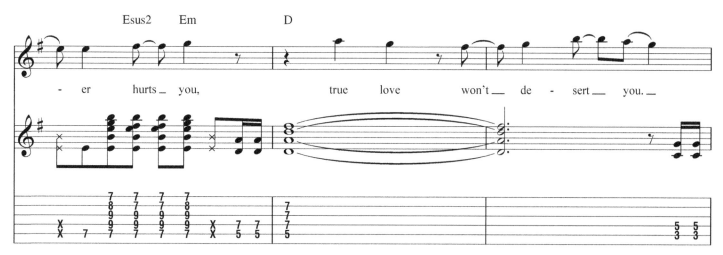

- er hurts _ you, true love won't __ de - sert __ you. __

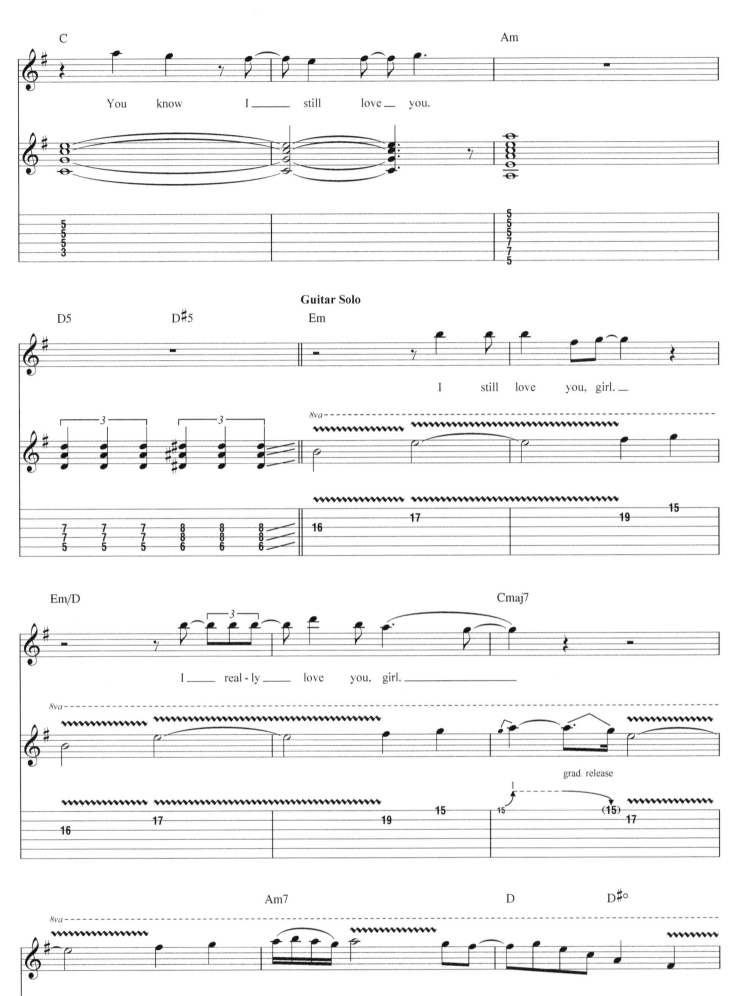

Additional Lyrics

Pre-Chorus If you must go, I wish you love.
You'll never walk alone.
Take care, my love.
Miss you, love.

You Give Love a Bad Name

Words and Music by Jon Bon Jovi, Desmond Child and Richie Sambora

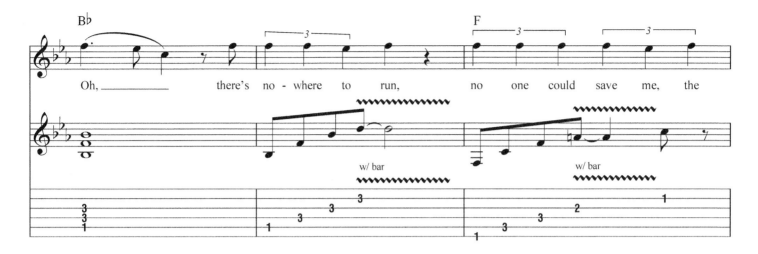

Oh, _____ there's no-where to run, no one could save me, the

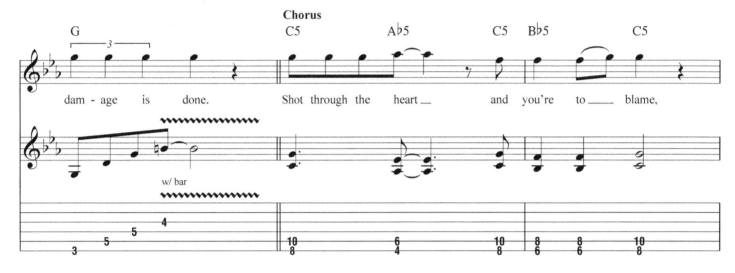

Chorus

dam - age is done. Shot through the heart __ and you're to __ blame,

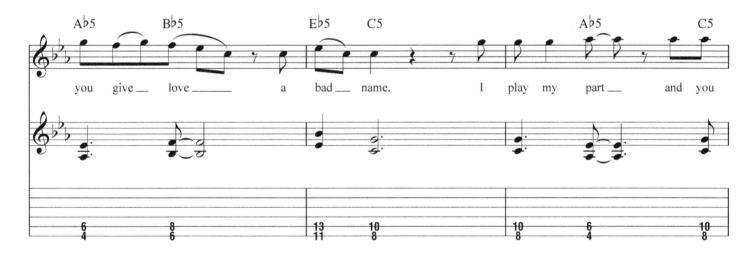

you give __ love __ a bad __ name. I play my part __ and you

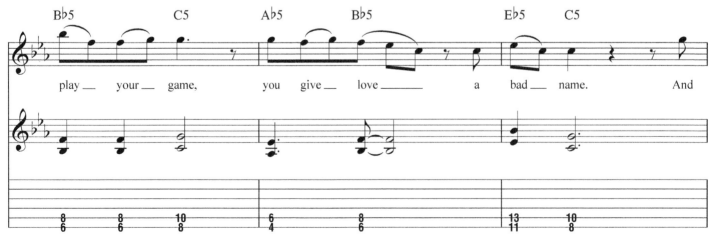

play __ your __ game, you give __ love __ a bad __ name. And

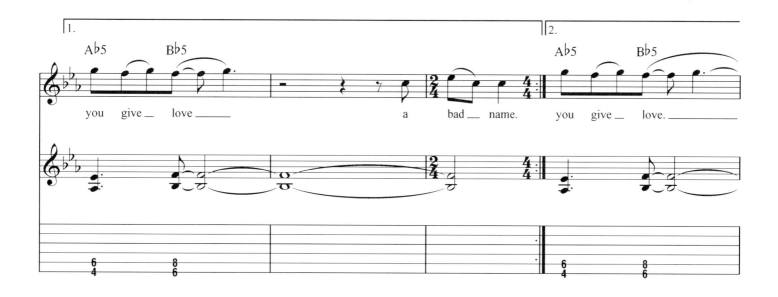

you give __ love _____ a bad __ name. you give __ love.

Guitar Solo

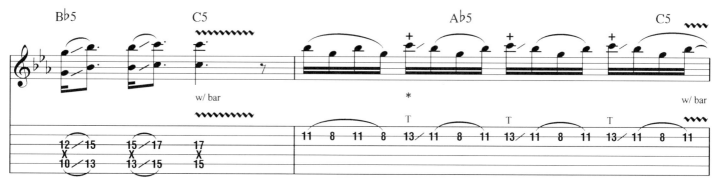

Whoa. __

*Tap & slide w/ edge of pick.

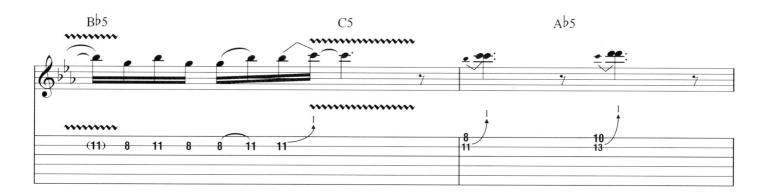

Breakdown-Chorus

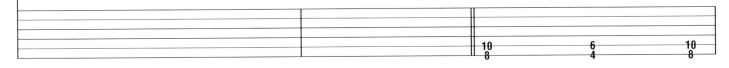

Shot through the heart ___ and you're to ___ blame, you give love ___ a

bad ___ name. I play my part ___ and you play ___ your ___ game,

Chorus

you give ___ love ___ a bad ___ name. Shot through the heart ___ and

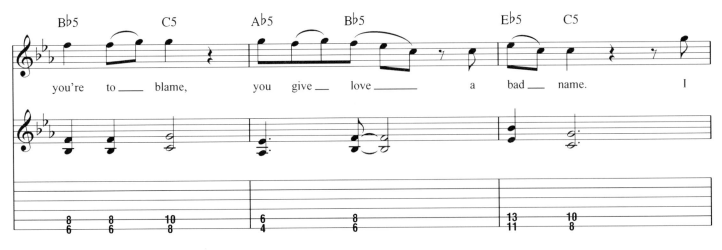

you're to ___ blame, you give ___ love ___ a bad ___ name. I

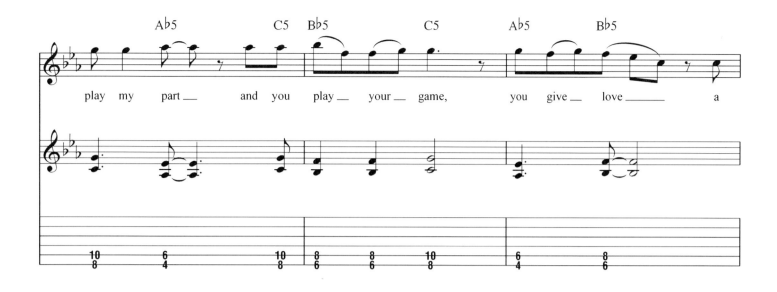

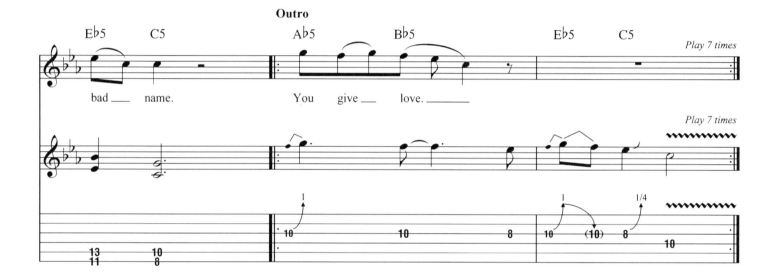

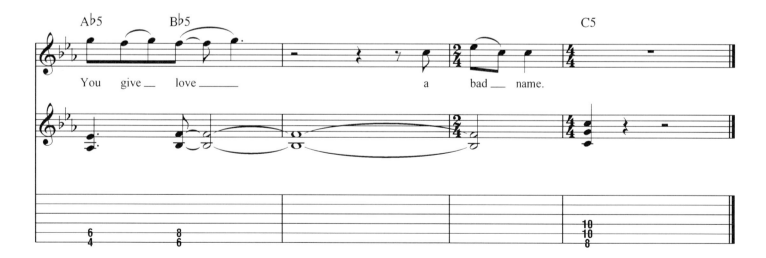

Additional Lyrics

2. You paint your smile on your lips.
Blood-red nails on your fingertips.
A school boy's dream, you act so shy.
Your very first kiss was your first kiss goodbye.

HAL·LEONARD GUITAR PLAY-ALONG

Complete song lists available online.

This series will help you play your favorite songs quickly and easily. Just follow the tab and listen to the audio to the hear how the guitar should sound, and then play along using the separate backing tracks. Audio files also include software to slow down the tempo without changing pitch. The melody and lyrics are included in the book so that you can sing or simply follow along. **INCLUDES TAB**

Prices, contents, and availability subject to change without notice.

HAL·LEONARD®
www.halleonard.com

0222
173